LIGHT ON THE PATH

Written down by
M.C.

1885

Edited and Reprinted by
YOGI PHILOSOPHY PUBLICATIONS

LIGHT ON THE PATH
Written down by
M.C.

Edited and Reprinted by
Yogi Philosophy Publications

This edition, 26 pages, published in May 2016 in
Totnes, Devon, UK.

M.C. is Mabel Collins (1851 – 1927)
"Light on the Path" was originally published in 1885

ISBN – 978-0-9934443-2-6

Humanity. 2 Philosophy. 3 Theosophy.
4. Spirituality.

Printed by Createspace

For additional information please e-mail:
Annekellyvoiceovers@yahoo.co.uk

"Light on the Path" is a must have for every faithful and dedicated student of Theosophy.

*"For when the disciple is ready,
the Master is ready also."*

"This little book—a true jewel—belongs to, and emanates from the same school of Indo-Aryan and Buddhist thought and learning as the teachings in "The Secret Doctrine.""

~ H.P. Blavatsky

Table of Contents

LIGHT ON THE PATH

A Treatise Written for the Personal Use of Those Who Are Ignorant of the Eastern Wisdom, and Who Desire to Enter Within Its Influence.

I.

These rules are written for all disciples: Attend you to them.

Before the eyes can see, they must be incapable of tears. Before the ear can hear, it must have lost its sensitiveness. Before the voice can speak in the presence of the Masters, it must have lost the power to wound. Before the soul can stand in the presence of the Masters, its feet must be washed in the blood of the heart.

1. Kill out ambition. [1]

[1] Ambition is the first curse: the great tempter of the man who is rising above his fellows. It is the simplest form of looking for reward. Men of intelligence and power are led away from their higher possibilities by it continually. Yet it is a necessary teacher. Its results turn to dust and ashes in the mouth; like death and estrangement it shows the man at last that to work for self is to work for disappointment. But though this first rule seems so simple and easy, do not quickly pass it by. For these vices of the ordinary man pass through a subtle transformation and reappear with changed aspect in the heart of the disciple. It is easy to say: I will not be ambitious; it is not so easy to say:

When the Master reads my heart, he will find it clean utterly. The pure artist who works for the love of his work is sometimes more firmly planted on the right road than the Occultist, who fancies he has removed his interest from self, but who has in reality only enlarged the limits of experience and desire, and transferred his interest to the things which concern his larger span of life. The same principle applies to the other two seemingly simple rules. Linger over them and do not let yourself be easily deceived by your own heart. For now, at the threshold, a mistake can be corrected. But carry it on with you and it will grow and come to fruition, or else you must suffer bitterly in its destruction.

2. Kill out desire of life.

3. Kill out desire of comfort.

4. Work as those work who are ambitious. Respect life as those do who desire it. Be happy as those are who live for happiness.

Seek in the heart the source of evil and expunge it. It lives fruitfully in the heart of the devoted disciple as well as in the heart of the man of desire. Only the strong can kill it out. The weak must wait for its growth, its fruition, its death. And it is a plant that lives and increases throughout the ages. It flowers when the man has accumulated unto himself innumerable existences. He who will enter upon the path of power must tear this thing out of his heart. And then the heart will bleed, and the whole life of the man seem to be utterly dissolved. This ordeal must be endured: it may come at the first step of the perilous ladder which leads to the path of life: it may not come until the last. But, O disciple, remember that it has to be endured, and fasten the energies of your soul upon the task. Live neither in the present nor the future, but in the Eternal. This giant weed cannot flower there: this blot upon existence is wiped out by the very atmosphere of eternal thought.

5. Kill out all sense of separateness. [2]

[2] Do not fancy you can stand aside from the bad man or the foolish man. They are yourself, though in a less degree than your friend or your Master. But if you allow the idea of separateness from any evil thing or person to grow up within you, by so doing you create karma, which will bind you to that thing or person till your soul recognizes that it cannot be isolated. Remember that the sin and shame of the world are your sin and shame; for you are a part of it; your karma is inextricably interwoven with the great Karma. And before you can attain knowledge you must have passed through all places, foul and clean alike. Therefore, remember that the soiled garment you shrink from touching may have been yours yesterday, and may be yours to-morrow. And if you

turn with horror from it, when it is flung upon your shoulders, it will cling the more closely to you. The self-righteous man makes for himself a bed of mire. Abstain because it is right to abstain—not that yourself shall be kept clean.

6. Kill out desire for sensation.

7. Kill out the hunger for growth.

8. Yet stand alone and isolated, because nothing that is embodied, nothing that is conscious of separation, nothing that is out of the Eternal, can aid you. Learn from sensation and observe it, because only so can you commence the science of self-knowledge, and plant your foot on the first step of the ladder. Grow as the flower grows, unconsciously, but eagerly anxious to open its soul to the air. So must you press forward to open your soul to the Eternal. But it must be the Eternal that draws forth your strength and beauty, not desire of growth. For in the one case you develop in the luxuriance of purity; in the other you harden by the forcible passion for personal stature.

9. Desire only that which is within you.

10. Desire only that which is beyond you.

11. Desire only that which is unattainable.

12. For within you is the light of the world—the only light that can be shed upon the Path. If you are unable to perceive it within you, it is useless to look for it elsewhere. It is beyond you, because when you reach it you have lost yourself. It is unattainable, because it forever recedes. You will enter the light, but you will never touch the Flame.

13. Desire power ardently.

14. Desire peace fervently.

15. Desire possessions above all.

16. But those possessions must belong to the pure soul only, and be possessed therefore by all pure souls equally, and thus be the especial property of the whole only when united. Hunger for such possessions as can be held by the pure soul, that you may accumulate wealth for that united spirit of life which is your only true self. The peace you shall desire is that sacred peace which nothing can disturb, and in which the soul grows as does the holy flower upon the still lagoons. And that power which the disciple shall covet is that which shall make him appear as nothing in the eyes of men.

17. Seek out the way. [3]

[3] These four words seem, perhaps, too slight to stand

alone. The disciple may say: “Should I study these thoughts at all; did I not seek out the way?” Yet do not pass on hastily. Pause and consider awhile. Is it the way you desire, or is it that there is a dim perspective in your visions of great heights to be scaled by yourself, of a great future for you to compass? Be warned. The way is to be sought for its own sake, not with regard to your feet that shall tread it.

There is a correspondence between this rule and the seventeenth of the second series. When after ages of struggle and many victories the final battle is won, the final secret demanded, then you are prepared for a further path. When the final secret of this great lesson is told, in it is opened the mystery of the new way—a path which leads out of all human experience, and which is utterly beyond human perception or imagination. At each of these points it is needful to pause long and consider well. At each of these points it is necessary to be sure that the way is chosen for its own sake. The way and the truth come first, then follows the life.

18. Seek the way by retreating within.

19. Seek the way by advancing boldly without.

20. Seek it not by any one road. To each temperament there is one road which seems the most

desirable. But the way is not found by devotion alone, by religious contemplation alone, by ardent progress, by self-sacrificing labor, by studious observation of life. None alone can take the disciple more than one step onward. All steps are necessary to make up the ladder. The vices of men become steps in the ladder, one by one, as they are surmounted. The virtues of man are steps indeed, necessary—not by any means to be dispensed with. Yet, though they create a fair atmosphere and a happy future, they are useless if they stand alone. The whole nature of man must be used wisely by the one who desires to enter the way. Each man is to himself absolutely the way, the truth, and the life. But he is only so when he grasps his whole individuality firmly, and, by the force of his awakened spiritual will recognizes this individuality as not himself, but that thing which he has with pain created for his own use, and by means of which he purposes, as his growth slowly develops his intelligence, to reach to the life beyond individuality. When he knows that for this his wonderful, complex, separated life exists, then, indeed, and then only, he is upon the way. Seek it by plunging into the mysterious and glorious depths of your own innermost being. "Recognize that every experience in life is a test, and utilize"* the senses in order to understand the growth and meaning of individuality, and the beauty and obscurity of those other divine fragments which are struggling side by side with you, and form the race to which you belong. Seek it by study of the laws of being, the laws of nature, the laws of the supernatural; and seek it by making the profound obeisance of the soul to the dim star that burns within. Steadily, as you watch and worship, its light will grow stronger. Then you may know you have found the beginning of the way. And when you have found the end, its light will suddenly become the infinite light. [4]

[4] "Recognize that all experience in life is a test," * and remember that when I say this I do not say: "Yield to the seductions of sense in order to know it." Before you have become an Occultist you may do this; but not afterwards. When you have chosen and entered the Path you cannot yield to these seductions without shame. Yet you can experience them without horror: can weigh, observe, and test them; and wait with the patience of confidence for the hour when they shall affect you no longer. But do not condemn the man that yields; stretch out your hand to him as a brother pilgrim whose feet have become heavy with mire. Remember, O disciple, that great though the gulf may be between the good man and the sinner, it is greater between the good man and the man who has attained knowledge; it is immeasurable between the good man and the one on the threshold of divinity. Therefore be wary lest too soon you fancy yourself a thing apart from the mass. When you have found the beginning of the way the star of your soul will show its light; and by that light you will perceive

how great is the darkness in which it burns. Mind, heart, brain, all are obscure and dark until the first great battle has been won. Be not appalled and terrified by the sight; keep your eyes fixed on the small light and it will grow. But let the darkness within help you to understand the helplessness of those who have seen no light, whose souls are in profound gloom. Blame them not, shrink not from them, but try to lift a little of the heavy karma of the world; give your aid to the few strong hands that hold back the powers of darkness from obtaining complete victory. Then do you enter into a partnership of joy, which brings indeed terrible toil and profound sadness, but also a great and ever-increasing delight.

* *Adaptation made by editor*

21. Look for the flower to bloom in the silence that follows the storm: not till then.

It shall grow, it will shoot up, it will make branches and leaves and form buds, while the storm continues, while the battle lasts. But not till the whole personality of the man is dissolved and melted—not until it is held by the divine fragment which has created it, as a mere subject for grave experiment and experience—not until the whole nature has yielded and become subject unto its higher self, can the bloom open. Then will come a calm such as comes in a tropical country after the heavy rain, when Nature works so swiftly that one may see her action. Such a calm will come to the harassed spirit. And in the deep silence the mysterious event will occur which will prove that the way has been found. Call it by what name you will, it is a voice that speaks where there is none to speak—it is a messenger that comes, a messenger without form or substance; or it is the flower of the soul that has opened. It cannot be described by any metaphor. But it can be felt after, looked for, and desired, even amid the raging of the storm. The silence may last a moment of time or it may last a thousand years. But it will end. Yet you will carry its strength with you. Again and again the battle must be fought and won. It is only for an interval that Nature can be still. [5]

[5] The opening of the bloom is the glorious moment when perception awakes: with it come confidence, knowledge, certainty. The pause of the soul is the moment of wonder, and the next moment of satisfaction, that is the silence.

Know, O disciple, that those who have passed through the silence: and felt its peace, and retained its strength; they long that you shall pass through it also. Therefore, in the Hall of Learning, when he is capable of entering there, the disciple will always find his Master.

Those that ask shall have. But though the ordinary

man asks perpetually, his voice is not heard. For he asks with his mind only; and the voice of the mind is only heard on that plane on which the mind acts. Therefore, not until the first twenty-one rules are passed do I say those that ask shall have.

To read, in the occult sense, is to read with the eyes of the spirit. To ask is to feel the hunger within—the yearning of spiritual aspiration. To be able to read means having obtained the power in a small degree of gratifying that hunger. When the disciple is ready to learn, then he is accepted, acknowledged, recognized. It must be so, for he has lit his lamp, and it cannot be hidden. But to learn is impossible until the first great battle has been won. The mind may recognize truth, but the spirit cannot receive it. Once having passed through the storm and attained the peace, it is then always possible to learn, even though the disciple waver, hesitate, and turn aside. The Voice of the Silence remains within him, and though he leave the Path utterly, yet one day it will resound and rend him asunder and separate his passions from his divine possibilities. Then, with pain and desperate cries from the deserted lower self, he will return.

Therefore I say, Peace be with you, "My peace I give unto you," can only be said by the Master to the beloved disciples who are as himself. There are some even among those who are ignorant of the Eastern wisdom to whom this can be said, and to whom it can daily be said with more completeness.

Δ Regard the three truths. They are equal.

These written above are the first of the rules which are written on the walls of the Hall of Learning. Those that ask shall have. Those that desire to read shall read. Those who desire to learn shall learn.

PEACE BE WITH YOU.

Δ

II.

Out of the silence that is peace a resonant voice shall arise. And this voice will say: It is not well; thou hast reaped, now thou must sow. And knowing this voice to be the silence itself thou wilt obey.

Thou who art now a disciple, able to stand, able to hear, able to see, able to speak; who hast conquered desire and attained to self-knowledge; who hast seen thy soul in its bloom and recognized it; and heard the Voice of the Silence, go thou to the Hall of Learning and read what is written there for thee. [6]

[6] To be able to stand is to have confidence; to be able to hear is to have opened the doors of the soul; to be able to see is to have attained perception; to be able to speak is to have attained the power of helping others; to have conquered desire is to have learned how to use and control the self; to have attained to self-knowledge is to have retreated to the inner fortress from whence the personal man can be viewed with impartiality; to have seen thy soul in its bloom is to have obtained a momentary glimpse in thyself of the transfiguration which shall eventually make thee more than man; to recognize is to achieve the great task of gazing upon the blazing light without dropping the eyes, and not falling back in terror, as

though before some ghastly phantom. This happens to some, and so when the victory is all but won it is lost; to hear the Voice of the Silence is to understand that from within comes the only true guidance; to go to the Hall of Learning is to enter the state in which learning becomes possible. Then will many words be written there for thee, and written in fiery letters for thee easily to read. For when the disciple is ready, the Master is ready also.

1. Stand aside in the coming battle, and though thou fightest be not thou the warrior.

2. Look for the Warrior and let him fight in thee.

3. Take his orders for battle and obey them.

4. Obey him, not as though he were a general, but as though he were thyself, and his spoken words were the utterance of thy secret desires; for he is thyself, yet infinitely wiser and stronger than thyself. Look for him, else in the fever and hurry of the fight thou mayest pass him; and he will not know thee unless thou knowest him. If thy cry meet his listening ear, then will he fight in thee, and fill the dull void within. And if this is so, then canst thou go through the fight cool and unwearied, standing aside and letting him battle for thee. Then it will be impossible for thee to strike one blow amiss. But if thou look not for him, if thou pass him by, then there is no safeguard for thee.

Thy brain will reel, thy heart grow uncertain, and in the dust of the battle-field thy sight and senses will fail, and thou wilt not know thy friends from thy enemies.

He is thyself. Yet thou art but finite and liable to error; he is eternal and is sure. He is eternal truth. When once he has entered thee and become thy Warrior, he will never utterly desert thee, and at the day of the great peace he will become one with thee.

5. Listen to the song of life. [7]

[7] Look for it, and listen to it, first in your own heart. At first you may say "It is not there; when I search I find only discord." Look deeper. If again you are disappointed, pause and look deeper again. There is a natural melody, an obscure fount in every human heart. It may be hidden over and utterly concealed and silenced—but it is there. At the very base of your nature you will find faith, hope, and love. He that chooses evil refuses to look within himself, shuts his ears to the melody of his heart, as he blinds his eyes to the light of his soul. He does this because he finds it easier to live in desires. But underneath all life is the strong current that cannot be checked; the great waters are there in reality. Find them, and you will perceive that none, not the most wretched of creatures, but is a part of it, however he blind himself to the fact and build up for himself a phantasmal

outer form of horror. In that sense it is that I say to you—All those beings among whom you struggle on are fragments of the Divine. And so deceptive is the illusion in which you live, that it is hard to guess where you will first detect the sweet voice in the hearts of others. But know that it is certainly within yourself. Look for it there, and once having heard it, you will more readily recognize it around you.

6. Store in your memory the melody you hear.

7. Learn from it the lesson of harmony.

8. You can stand upright now, firm as a rock amid the turmoil, obeying the Warrior who is thyself and thy king. Unconcerned in the battle save to do his bidding, having no longer any care as to the result of the battle, for one thing only is important, that the warrior shall win, and you know he is incapable of defeat—standing thus, cool and awakened, use the hearing you have acquired by pain and by the destruction of pain. Only fragments of the great song come to your ears while yet you are but man. But if you listen to it, remember it faithfully, so that none which has reached you is lost, and endeavour to learn from it the meaning of the mystery which surrounds you. In time you will need no teacher. For as the individual has voice, so has that in which the individual exists. Life itself has speech and is never silent. And its utterance is not, as you that are deaf

may suppose, a cry: it is a song. Learn from it that you are part of the harmony; learn from it to obey the laws of the harmony.

9. Regard earnestly all the life that surrounds you.

10. Learn to look intelligently into the hearts of men. [8]

[8] From an absolutely impersonal point of view, otherwise your sight is coloured. Therefore impersonality must first be understood.

Intelligence is impartial: no man is your enemy: no man is your friend. All alike are your teachers. Your enemy becomes a mystery that must be solved, even though it take ages: for man must be understood. Your friend becomes a part of yourself, an extension of yourself, a riddle hard to read. Only one thing is more difficult to know—your own heart. Not until the bonds of personality are loosed can that profound mystery of self begin to be seen. Not till you stand aside from it will it in any way reveal itself to your understanding. Then, and not till then, can you grasp and guide it. Then, and not till then, can you use all its powers, and devote them to a worthy service.

11. Regard most earnestly your own heart.

12. For through your own heart comes the one light which can illuminate life and make it clear to your eyes.

Study the hearts of men; that you may know what is that world in which you live and of which you will to be a part. Regard the constantly changing and moving life which surrounds you, for it is formed by the hearts of men; and as you learn to understand their constitution and meaning, you will by degrees be able to read the larger word of life.

13. Speech comes only with knowledge. Attain to knowledge and you will attain to speech. [9]

[9] It is impossible to help others till you have obtained some certainty of your own. When you have learned the first twenty-one rules and have entered the Hall of Learning with your powers developed and sense unchained, then you will find there is a fount within you from which speech will arise.

After the thirteenth rule I can add no words to what is already written.

MY PEACE I GIVE UNTO YOU.

Δ

These notes are written only for those to whom I give my peace; those who can read what I have written with the inner as well as the outer sense.

14. Having obtained the use of the inner senses, having conquered the desires of the outer senses,

having conquered the desires of the individual soul, and having obtained knowledge, prepare now, O disciple, to enter upon the way in reality. The path is found: make yourself ready to tread it.

15. Inquire of the earth, the air, and the water, of the secrets they hold for you. The development of your inner senses will enable you to do this.

16. Inquire of the Holy Ones of the earth of the secrets they hold for you. The conquering of the desires of the outer senses will give you the right to do this.

17. Inquire of the inmost, the One, of its final secret which it holds for you through the ages.

The great and difficult victory, the conquering of the desires of the individual soul, is a work of ages; therefore expect not to obtain its reward until ages of experience have been accumulated. When the time of learning this seventeenth rule is reached, man is on the threshold of becoming more than man.

18. The knowledge which is now yours is only yours because your soul has become one with all pure souls and with the inmost. It is a trust vested in you by the Most High. Betray it, misuse your knowledge, or neglect it, and it is possible even now for you to fall from the high estate you have attained. Great ones

fall back, even from the threshold, unable to sustain the weight of their responsibility, unable to pass on. Therefore look forward always with awe and trembling to this moment, and be prepared for the battle.

19. It is written that for him who is on the threshold of divinity no law can be framed, no guide can exist. Yet to enlighten the disciple, the final struggle may be thus expressed:

Hold fast to that which has neither substance nor existence.

20. Listen only to the voice which is soundless.

21. Look only on that which is invisible alike to the inner and the outer sense.

PEACE BE WITH YOU.

Δ

Printed in Great Britain
by Amazon

44879187R00018